The BEST AMERICAN EMAILS

Collected with help from Russia's finest hackers.

Edited by Amanda Meadows

THE
DEVASTATOR

LOS ANGELES

D1076964

Written by
Amanda Meadows

Editor
Geoffrey Golden

Cover Design by Geoffrey Golden

"Family Christmas" photo by Breezy Baldwin on Flickr

Copyright © 2017 Amanda Meadows

First Edition: June 2017

ISBN-13: 978-1-942099-23-9 | ISBN-10: 1-942099-23-1

devastatorpress.com

PRINTED IN ~~AN OFFSHORE SERVER FARM~~ KOREA

Contents

"The greatest form of communication
is the email."

–Ray Tomlinson, creator of the email

Foreword

Like many of you, I've spent over 20 years reading and writing emails. But unlike you, I am a famous author and critic of the written word, so my opinion means so much more than yours. I've sent emails to family, to strangers online, to colleagues at work, to the longtime subscribers of my newsletter on healthy and sustainable living.

When I go to the occasional literary function, I am enraged to find that the majority of my peers – these so-called people of letters – ignore the quotidian poignancy of the email! Seriously, what's up with that?

While there are billions of emails in cyberspace, the literary email circle is quite small. When I ran into dear friend and colleague, George Meyershaw, at the Em@ily Awards ceremony, he showed me his humblest work yet: an out-of touch complaint email to a local cable company. He asked, "Does this capture the cultural cluelessness of the Baby Boomer white male, while betraying a whiff of his fearful devotion to the capitalist framework?" My answer was, of course, yes and yes. It was included in this very volume.

Join me in a celebration of these tiny triumphs of human frailty and pettiness, of delusion and desperation. The inbox, she is deep. There are much further depths to plumb, and more attachments to scan for viruses.

Best in eCommerce

The internet sales world is built on emails: Newsletters, order confirmations, shipping confirmations, delivery confirmations, return confirmations, receipt of return confirmations, customer service complaint confirmations, customer service response notifications, public shaming of company's customer service response on social media, Medium.com think piece on the customer service scandal, backlash on customer inciting customer service scandal, customer changing name and moving to Canada to start a new life using a Zappos.ca account. The cycle is sacred.

[DealTime] Our Mom's Imaginary Cat Friend Likes These Deals

To: *waytogotommy@mac.com*

From: *dealtimedeals@dealtime.deals*

Subject: [DealTime] Our Mom's Imaginary Cat Friend Likes These Deals

WOW! DEALTIME Y'ALL!

THESE DEALS ARE FOR...

L33T H4X0Rs ONLY!

6% off Thai Appetizers from 3pm-5pm

$60 for $45 worth of atomic buffalo wings at Wings4Mouth

Buy 2 get 50% free at OnlyToddlerSocks (not good for infant sizes)

FREE 4-minute couples massage at Thai Me Up, Thai Me Down Spa. Excludes oils.

40% off spin classes for dogs at City BarkBikes!

$12 off scalp removal at LUXE LaserBangs

FREE shipping on your next merkin from OvernightMerkins.com

2% off unlimited "dumpster dibs" membership at Freegan Grocery Warehouse

Follow us for more deals on <u>Peach</u>!

Deals only available between 1pm-4pm on 2/23. Redeem deals with the DealTime app, but only if downloaded to every device in household. No deals are valid.

<u>Forward this to your 10 cheapest and least discriminatory acquaintances</u>

<u>Unsubscribe</u>

Alert! You Left Something in Your Cart 3 Years Ago

To: *darryljenkins@hotmail.com*
From: *ggecustomerservice@gge.com*
Subject: Alert! You Left Something in Your Cart 3 Years Ago

Hey [Darryl],

Uh oh! Looks like you left this in your cart:

Description: Tommy Hilfiger "Holder" duffel bag
Color: appropriate
Size: big
Material: yes

Speaking of your shopping cart, we have a new website! Have you seen the slicker side of General Goods Emporium?

Click here to take a tour of our new crib! That's still cool, right? "Cribs?"

Things are bad here, man. Bad! You don't even know what I've seen. Each day, we wake up and pray that you'll come back to your cart. Will you, please?

We'll be honest. If you don't come back and buy this duffel bag, we're going to file for Chapter 11 bankruptcy. Do you really want that on your hands? Think about this.

Help us out. Come on. You're not a monster, right?

Oh god. I'm getting fired. Fuck. This happened to me at Groupon, too. Fuck!

Buy the bag!

Unsubscribe from General Goods Emporium

Receive double the emails from General Goods Emporium

Etsy Conversation with sweetvalentine23

To: *nuthinbunttruble@gmail.com*
From: *support@etsy.com*
Subject: Etsy Conversation with sweetvalentine23

Hi NuthinBuntTruble,

Sorry, but my bunting order arrived and it wasn't of the "premium bunting" standard that was promised. Despite your claims of "buntiful" amounts of pennants, There were too few "bunts" on my premium burlap bunting.

I had a beautiful barn wedding and your frankly embarrassing attempt at "bunting" ruined the entire evening. I submitted photos to the super popular wedding blog Something Borrowed, Something Bunted and they did *not* feature it! The reason, I assume, is because the "bunting" was not as "on point" as you claimed it would be. I'm hemorrhaging Pinterest followers!

For added insult, my new mother-in-law comes from a long line of bunters and I was terribly embarrassed! After pressing my new husband several times, he admitted it set our marriage on the wrong foot and now he is having doubts.

Without bunting, we have nothing.

I would send the bunting back for an Etsy Bunting Refund, except we left the bunting at the site and forgot about it. If you expect me to drive all the way to a barn in Chesterton, Virginia just to retrieve your substandard bunting, you are a worse Etsy Seller than I thought !!

At this point, I can't get a refund on our wedding, either – the wedding insurance doesn't cover bad bunting! My next email is to the wedding insurance company, because this is simply madness.

I will be expecting a PayPal from you IMMEDIATELY, along with a handcrafted artisanal apology.

Sincerely disappointed,

sweetvalentine23

Best in Work

From the rat race to the corner office, work is where emails are the most mandatory and pointlessness at once. Office emails are an inextinguishable evil and we deserve what we have created. The following are the most grating examples.

Content Warning: the idea of working; being at work.

Real quick

To: *bradframingham@gmail.com*
From: *brad.no.50@weconnect.com*
Subject: Real quick

Hey Brad F.!

Sup, man. Thanks again for being so chill about the new desk sharing rules at WeConnect, California's #1 co-working and Apple product charging space. Our co-working spaces are meant to be hubs for collaboration.

That said, did you check out the Slack channel? I think there might be a miscommunication.

We're all about collaboration and sharing – that's the whole vibe here! However, our policy is that desks can be split in half, **but** those halves can't also be split. So, no quarters. That also, unfortunately, means you cannot then split those quarters into 8ths, or split those 8ths into 16ths, amigo.

There is a photo circulating in the admin's office of one 4 foot desk with 24 laptops on it. Not sure how everyone is sitting? You guys are so creative!

Anyway my man, splitting your desk into 16ths and subletting them simultaneously is not only against our policy, but breeds disease. Someone sneezed last week and three people died by EOD. Their desk space was auctioned off to the Waitlist, and the unidentified freelancers' bodies were cremated. You can find their remains next to that one Keurig we have provided for all two hundred of you.

Bro, if you can't handle the current sitch, no worries! We can always move you to the $40/month "Bathroom Use Only" plan.

But make sure you hit us up before the end of the month, dude – no one wants to incur the late payment penalty of telling everyone that you still have an iPhone 5.

Hope this helps!

Brad D.
WeConnect Support
Try "The Un-Office"

(No Subject)

To: *info@watchesmonthly.org*
From: *morgant94@ymail.com*
Subject: (No Subject)

Hello To Whom It May Concern,

Hope this finds you well. My name is Morgan Thomlinson and I am emailing to inquire regarding the important position of editorial intern for *WATCHES Monthly*, as it relevant to my various skillsets.

I am indubitably excited to share with you my extensive expertise in the reading and writing arena. I am a student at American Eagle University of South Eastern Kansas and about to graduate with a 3.1 GPA in Cover Letter Studies.

When my grandfather died in my arms, he left behind a one of his more precious effects: a pocketwatch. Since then, timepieces and time recording equipment have been a passion of mine.

I was an indispensible member of the American Eagle University of South Eastern Kansas debate team, where I have debated on important topics such as abortion, legalized marijuana, and the Rapture. I have found watches to be surpassingly useful for being on time to practices, debates, and the club's social gatherings – and that is not up for debate! I have also been an integral part of

American Eagle's Gold Key Honors Society, and the Drama department, where our plays incorporate watches stored in the costume department with the utmost regularity.

In addition: I was a Trainee Hostess at Applebee's in the prestigious Hostess Trainee Program, which was in the same plaza as a watch repair shop. This period was an indispensible time in my life – vitally so.

It would be at my utmost pleasure to serve you and your staff. Attached is my resume, and my most recent school paper on the importance of the sun dial.

Would I be a prominent benefit to your organization? Only "time" will tell! (Feel free to use that if you would like!)

Sincerely yours to hire,

Morgan Tomlinson
Student and Prospective Employee

Position Available: Jobware Tempsources #82696852354

To: *tomkrugman@gmail.com*

From: *lpiper@recuiting.biz*

Subject: Position Available: Jobware Tempsources #82696852354

My name is Linda Piper and I'm a Senior Recruiter at Jobware Tempsources. Jobware Tempsources is seeking a Content Sales Rockstar for challenging, rewarding work in Simi Valley, CA. If you have ALL the required skills and experience noted below, please save your updated resume as a WordPerfect file along with the hourly pay rate you are willing to settle for in a separate WordPerfect file.

Job Title: Content Sales Rockstar

Duration: 1 month(s) with the potential to be shortened

Location: On-site in Simi Valley, CA

IMPORTANT: MUST KNOW ADOBE PREMIER, ADOBE LIGHT SHOP, FINAL CUT PRO, EXCEL TEMPSHEETS, SALESFORCE, SODASHOP PRO, RECONPLUS, SHARPIMAGE+, BURGERTIME, AND COWCITYCODER.

Responsibilities:

- Conceptualize what this position should be
- Working closely with ideation team to click "yes" on Google Calendar invites
- Proactively engage in coffee acquisition
- Enthusiastically engage in sexual partnerships with key content members of rival firm to tear apart from inside
- Proactively engage in time-based group conferences (also known as "meetings")
- Engage in engagement strategies
- Create fun work environment, as current work environment is a siege of never-ending hell fire

You Must Be:

- Able to memorize all sitcom catchphrases to fill in long gaps in conversation
- Hang-loose enthusiast (rival firm uses "thumbs up")
- Into close talking
- Able to attach cat GIFs to all emails
- Willing to lose everything

If you have 15 years of relevant experience and are available, interested, around, ready to make a new start in your life, ready to plan to make a change; or know of a friend who might fit the required criteria and is interested in working in a relaxed, high-intensity work environment, please reply – even if we have spoken recently about a different position, if you have asked me not to email you again, or even if you are recently deceased. Perhaps a relative at your funeral services has the above qualifications?

If you do respond via e-mail please include a daytime phone number, so I can also call you every day for the next 6 months. Please remember to respond ASAP.

All the best,

Linda Piper

This email was written in WordPerfect!

Best in Dad
Telling It Like It Is

A father of any gender is an invaluable source of unsolicited wisdom. Sometimes a father's (lack of) encouragement is what makes the difference in a child's life (therapy bills). These emails showcase fathers brimming with good intentions and not much else.

Sunday Call?

To: *daniel.p87@gmail.com*
From: *geraldp@earthlink.net*
Subject: Sunday Call?

Hi there Daniel,

Wanted to to check in and see when are you coming back to Westchester next. This Monday the 15th will be 46 degrees, and Tuesday the 16th will be 32 degrees. Just thought you should know, since you always ask about the weather!

You should also know that your Godfather Mr. Forrester died this week at 97 years young. It came as a surprise – he was just about to be transferred to hospice next week. Luckily, the service will cost as much as the hospice would have, and that's a one-time expense. Lucky guy.

Do you remember my canasta buddy Perry Danforth? He was the one with the bifocals at the table. You met him once when you were 12, I want to say when the game was at our house that one time because Alvin Minkle's furnished basement flooded. He talked about you every day ever since. Well, he died, too. And so did Alvin Minkle. They were both hit by the same bus. It was the Local #3 Southbound on Harris Blvd. (At different times, if you can believe it! They didn't fire the bus driver – he and the head of the Transit Authority are old army buddies.) Very sad.

Can you tell your sister that her 4th grade teacher Mrs. Barrington also died? She was shoveling snow along Harris Blvd. You know, the road where the #3 goes by. Please tell your sister for me.

All right, call me this Sunday and we can talk about when you're going to come visit. Just call before 3pm, because I'll be at a funeral at 4, and another one at 6:30. After that, your mother and I will be busy picking our cemetery plots.

Lots of love,

Dad

http://www.theonion.com/ news/area-man-tired- burrito-54800

To: *leslie.thomas@gmail.com*

From: *papahenry@yahoo.com*

Subject: http://www.theonion.com/news/area-man-tired-burrito-54800

HI LESLIE,

I watched your YOUTUBE video skit. It was pretty good. However: Do all your skits have to be about your vagina? You know, Rita Rudner doesn't have to do that!

Have you ever heard of a website called THE ONION? It's actually quite funny. You should ask to work there.

Did you see my other email about BARACKOBAMAJOKES. COM ? Also good!

BEST,

DAD

PS: You should tell the director that the doctor's chair in the video was the wrong kind for a dentist's office. Maybe he can go back and fix it.

Best in Momspiration

Mothers provide 89% of America's emails. They work tirelessly to keep their children safe, educated, and up-to-date on who your 3rd cousin just married. These great Momspiration emails reminds one of their roots, keeping one's head high and eyes widely rolled.

Coming Home?

To: *floraforever@gmail.com*
From: *sandra_lewis@aol.com*
Subject: Coming Home?

Flora! We're so looking forward to you coming home from the big apple! I love you and I'm very PROUD of you achieving your dreams of being able to afford a tiny apartment!

I wanted to make sure you saw that flights are CHEAP to Minneapolis for August next year. Don't wait until the last minute again to buy a ticket. It's *always really nice* out in the middle of August.

We could go to the Structure Garden together!! So many structures. It's wonderful to live here.

Remember my friend Marcia's son Rikard? He's so kind, and he has that distinctive laugh! I already told them you were coming. You can't make an excuse this time – when you went home early last Christmas, Rikard checked your Facebook and there was NO MENTION of any kind of dog emergency.

So please do not EMBARRASS me again regarding Rikard. Marcia's in charge of the bridge club.

And honey here's a clip of Alex Jones DEFINITIVELY explaining how fluoridated water is a government program paid for by that darned George Soros, to make us sympathize with illegal immigrants:

http://garf.info/gfyw

So can we stop debating? Mom won the arguement!

Xxxxxxxx

Momma

PS: Rikard had his leg braces removed last fall, and Marcia wants to make sure you knew that before you back out.

PPS: Rikard says hi!

Hi from Mommy

To: *jessek83@gmail.com, jenniferk86@gmail.com*
From: *debbiek62@yahoo.com*
Subject: Hi from Mommy

Hi kids !

Here's a really nice poem I found ~very~ inspiring …… !

KINDNESS IS A CHOICE
YOU CAN BE ~KIND~
BUT THAT DOESN'T MEAN
THAT KINDNESS
WILL COME BACK TO YOU
BECAUSE KINDNESS
TOUCHES YOUR SHOULDER
LIKE A MIRACLE
FILLING YOUR BOSOM
KINDNESS IS
CALLING BACK YOUR MOM
BECAUSE MOM NEEDS
TO PUT GRANDMA
INTO A HOME

xoxoxoxo
Mommy
555-6849 in case you forgot or lost your phone again!!

Best in Relationships

Email communication penetrates (see what I did there?) every important moment of life, from the first innocent invite to a coffee date to the first loathsome invite to a coffee shop to discuss the terms of the divorce. When the heat of romance meets the chill of an email, it creates a feeling of vague nausea in these world-class selections.

[WhyNotDate] Message from h0rnDADDY43

To: *mirandalovescake@gmail.com*
From: *whynotdate@wnd.com*
Subject: [WhyNotDate] Message from h0rnDADDY43

 You have a new message from h0rnDADDY43!

h0rnDADDY43

4% Hot Match | 73% Sworn Enemy
7% Chance You Haven't Given Up on Love Yet

Hi there m'lady I think you're pretty and could very well be the perfect womyn for me! Some info on me: I'm a metal guy, as in I both listen to and hump in rhythm to metal. I'm a big hugger, even though my mates give me grief about it (hehe). Oh, and I am very into the ART of body modification. Full disclosure: I am a horned human, with tentacle features. Also one of my kidneys is now a horn. I'm very much into the Horn Boi scene, with many of my friends also being Soldiers of the Bone.

If you're into the mod scene too, give me a yar! I love a lass with scaled skin or a sealed crack, but if you are willing to get zipper lips, even better!

From your photo, it seems as though you've had a breast augmentation. Personally, for me, women should be natural and celebrate their natural gifts, not overwrite them under a hot knife. You either got it or you don't, babe.

I obviously have very strict standards. If you ever touched my rough, realistic goat horns, which took me years to *mold, sand, and texture,* you would understand.

Also, did you know women that have gotten breast implants are much more likely to kill themselves? It's a fact, look it up.

Welp, I hope you are having a good night and that someone finally decides you are worth loving as you are – even though in your case, I think that would be impossible.

HAIL SATAN!

There are (1836) messages in your WhyNotDate inbox. Sign in to WhyNotDate immediately!

WEDDING INFO: V IMPORTANT! <3

To: *weddingpeeps@googlegroups.com*
From: *masonandbrieinatree@icloud.com*
Subject: WEDDING INFO: V IMPORTANT! <3

Hi Everyone We Love All in One Beautiful Email!

As you know, our wedding is this weekend! Here's everything you need to know:

1. Our ceremony will take place in a beautiful barn with lots of rustic decor. Be sure to wear comfortable shoes – cowboy boots for extra points! ;-) (Neiman Marcus has some really cute ones!)

2. The barn is legit rustic! Buuut the downside is the barn's also full of rusty nails, bugs, and stray varmints. Please take care to get a tetanus shot and a rabies shot. Also have a shot... of moonshine! ;-) Williams Sonoma has amazeballs moonshine.

3. THIS IS A SUGAR-FREE WEDDING. Mason and I have been on an enlightening macrobiotic cleanse and it changed our lives. Since we are having this wedding to share our lives with you, we insist you share in our lifestyle for just one sacred night. <3

4. Again, there will be NO cake or desserts. Please respect our

wishes. And don't smuggle in sweets! A little bird told me some of you were thinking of bringing donuts, but if you do, Mason and I will cry. ;-)

5. Back to the Barn! There <u>will</u> be heavy machinery and animal traps abound. We know – very authentic! The farmers we rented the space from were very "real!" We will use lots of cute burlap bunting as a cute form of "caution tape" to keep you from venturing near body-mangling farm equipment. :-D

6. We're so excited to share that our mutual best friend Trystan will be our officiant. He has zero experience with public speaking but a lifetime of experience... loving us. ;-) He's easily startled, though, so please don't clap!

7. Speaking of mutual friends: The farmers warned us about Ol' Tilda, the barn's ghost. Cool, right? Ol' Tilda's been haunting the barn for 245 years, so we thought it only fitting to incorporate her into the ceremony with an "old mother's wail" ritual! Such a sweet and very real ritual! :-O

8. How about some fun?! As you arrive, you will be greeted at a chicken coop. You will be asked to name and slaughter your own chicken! How sweet, right? Please bring a list of preferred chicken names so we can start on time. Chicken names that are already taken: Tatum, Cleo, Eloise, Benji, Aiden, Tycho, Emma, and Beckett. :-D

9. This is a "no phones" wedding! Please do not bring your phones at all. The barn is approx. 50 miles from the nearest highway, so be sure to print out your directions! If you must

bring your cell phone, check it in with our Wedding Blacksmith, who will destroy it for you. ;-)

10. We will have a Rustic Restroom. When you need to use the restroom, simply ask the Elder by the entryway, who will lead you to an outhouse. If the outhouse is occupied, there will be a complementary hole in the ground 10 feet from the outhouse. Bring your own wiping implements! Note: We are giving artisanal kerchiefs to each guest, but please DO NOT use them for this purpose! ;-O

11. Our hashtag is #BarningLove. Be sure to use it for everything you post on social media, so we can track who broke our no-phones rule! ;-)

12. Also please sign this waiver that every photo you take at our wedding belongs to #BarningLove, LLC. That's right, we incorporated our wedding to protect our budding new family's brand! Please respect our wishes and our sacred corporate personhood. ;-P

13. Remember to HAVE FUN this weekend! We made this event for YOU, the friends and family we love. ;-)

Remember to call our wedding planner Reaghan McNally (234-555-9463) if you have any questions, concerns, or panic attacks!

LOVE YOU!
Mason + Brie
Joint CEOs
#BarningLove, LLC.

Best in Breakups

It is true, love fades over time. Nearly every relationship fails – due to cheating, poor taste in music, death, and most commonly, the children. These emails showcase the pain and the desperation during and after a nasty breakup. Here's to the sad, bitter, and horny 99.99%.

Custody Mediation for Gary

To: *dantheman@hotmail.com*
From: *brendag24@mac.com*
Subject: Custody Mediation for Gary

Dan:

I'm done! I'm done! Why can't we just wrap up this divorce? Why are you avoiding the process server?

I know why: Gary. Don't think for a second I don't realize that our bird – no, MY bird, is why you're playing petty with me. Well, this African Grey Parrot doesn't want anything to with you, because you don't want anything to do with this Caucasian Grey Woman anymore.

When Gary says, "Gary wants a cracker," he's talking about the Cracker Barrel across the parkway from my apartment complex. And when Gary says, "What a fucking bastard, what a fucking bastard!" You know who he's talking about? YOU. These are facts. Gary knows over 99 words and YOUR NAME ISN'T ONE OF THOSE WORDS.

Gary made his choice. LIVE WITH IT.

Sincerely NOT yours*,

Brenda
* and neither is Gary!

Hey

To: *lovelyerin234@gmail.com*
From: *danielKisOK@gmail.com*
Subject: Hey

Hi Erin,

How are you these days? I thought I'd run into you at Brian's thing last month, but I guess you were too busy lolololol.

Listen, I know you're still pissed about how things ended. No one feels worse than I do. The thing is, I was really stressed out with work during those months, and scared of how deep my emotions were for you.

But, like, the sex was really good, right?

SO let's say I apologized – not that I am right now – IF I apologized, wouldn't it be really cool if we hooked up one more time, for the memories?

IF I said I was sorry for reading your emails while you showered, would you let me suck on your toes – just once more?

IF I said I was sorry for calling your dad and asking him why you had "so many daddy issues," would you let me finger you in a Buffalo Wild Wings again? That was our place.

IF I said I was sorry for having that secret sex condo with my bros, would you let me come in your hair?

Please hear me out, this is just a thought experiment. Like OJ Simpson's excellent and thought-provoking book, *If I Did It*.

Closure. That's what I'm offering us right now. Humor me.

Have sex with me. In *theory*.

Tempting, right?

Anyway, please get back to me as soon as you can! I'm sure your tits look super great still!

Possibly with love?

Daniel

Best in Friendship

Friends are life's best feature. Though, seriously: If they're really your friend, why are you emailing them? Is your phone in rice? If so: Have you waited 5 days? You can't just put your phone in rice for a couple of hours and then give up; that's not letting the rice activate its full power. I had a friend once who straight-up left her iPhone 6 in rice for a whole week, and when she took it out... no joke, it was a 7.

Cop Some New Air Force Ones?!

To: *jareds.email@gmail.com*

From: *mcohen@emory.edu*

Subject: Cop Some New Air Force Ones?!

Hey Bro!

Good seeing you at Dave's party! I've always thought we should hang out more. Super sorry I thought you were Jamal at first. I mean, I've never actually met a Jamal, so it's weird that I thought you were him, but uh, weird, right?

I saw that documentary about sneakerheads and went DEEP into sneakerhead culture! Now I'm a HUGE sneakerhead. Now I'm just like you, my BSF: Best Sneaker Friend!

You hear about Undefeated dropping the new Bape x Air Force One collabo? I heard about it on NPR's dope segment about Worldstar.

Also, like, you're probably used to being around other sneakerheads overnight more than I am, right? I was thinking we could wait in line together! I can bring some snacks. Can you bring your gat or knife or something? Like for protection? Tell me how I should "strap." GAT GAT GAT bruh!

Matt

PS: What's a good shoelace cleaner? Or, can you clean them for me?

Hello from Spiderman

To: *spideyfans@googlegroups.com*
From: *spiderman.azzedine86@gmail.com*
Subject: Hello from Spiderman

Hey pals! Heads up that my email address and contact info has changed. My name has legally changed to Spiderman Azzedine and my new email is spiderman.azzedine86@gmail.com.

It's really not a big deal, don't worry about it. I am NOT accepting any questions at this time. Please do your best to forget any previous name I may have had.

OK. Yes there is a story, but no time for that! Let's just say, after I broke things off with my "Mary Jane," I decided to web-sling over to city hall and deal with a major crisis... a mid-life crisis.

Buy me a drink some time and I might tell you more ;-) Anyway please add my new email to your contacts!

Yours,
Spidey

PS - Yes, I am available to dress as Spider-Man for your child's birthday party.

Best in Spam, International

We all like to believe that our first encounters with people from far away nations and cultures will be romantic, full of international intrigue and colorful scarves. In real life, only 29% of Americans will ever leave the country, so statisically, your most likely experience with foreign lands will be getting your identity stolen by Russian hackers.

MAN Samples

To: *tomlewis@yahoo.com*
From: *manblasters@ytmnd.ru*
Subject: MAN Samples

GET YOUR ELONGATING MAGIC DONE

FAST FAST FAST? TIME FOR MOIST CARESSES

SPECIAL FOR MALES TO USE ONLY WITH FEMALE

BUY HERE

у вас есть сдать всю информацию мне. У меня есть все ваши
контактные и вид на жительство информации. не колеблясь,
раскрывать с российскими официальными лицами в кремле.
купить все таблетки Дика или вы будете сталкиваться
следствию.

[Editor's translation: You have surrender all information to me.
I have all of your contact and residence information. Will not
hesitate to disclose with russian officials in kremlin. Buy all dick
pills or you will face consequence.]

Life Love in You

To: *bgranger@aol.com*
From: *lovelywoman@sexy.ru*
Subject: Life love in you

Good day my dear stranger How are you? I'm Darijah. I'm a free lady. Have own motor scooter. I am 41 today. I want to create committed relationship with good person.

If you become interested and need good love couple relations for create serious courtship you can answer to me.

In my message I am forwarding picture. Do you like picture? Very sexy. Can give for you more picture. Simple funds transfer and more picture.

I am waiting your letter.

See you later gator,,,,

Darijah

Не отвечайте женщине, она мешает, чтобы шантажировать вас. Привет, я российский диссидент, который пытается уничтожить Кремль. Вы можете следить за моей анонимной учетной записью Twitter @spyguy69, а также следить за моей поездкой. В любом случае, пожалуйста, не отвечайте, независимо от того, насколько вы возбудительны.

[Editor's translation: Do not respond to woman, she is honeytrap to blackmail you. Hi, I am a Russian dissident who is trying to take down the Kremlin. You might want to follow my anonymous twitter account @spyguy69 as well to follow my journey. Anyway, please do not respond, no matter how horny you are.]

Best in Spam, U.S.

When we think of spam, we tend to think of other countries grifting us from afar. But truly, some of the best scams come from the homefront. These emails best represent the entrepreneurial lure and junky pleasure of American spam.

Invoice Due Now, 3023YT45Q

To: *mandybaby134@yahoo.com*
From: *notascam@ads4ever.info*
Subject: Invoice Due Now, 3023YT45Q

Hello   ,,,

You have outstanding invoice as per fax #275-264HFSK.

Please pay now or computer will self-destruct, **BIG TIME!**.

Very serious! You payment is due now.

Payment due: $126,000,973 USD

Due date: NOW

We know your middle name is Barbara. See how real we are? Send to: ifsslav_re@us.ru

Computer self-destructing in 4…

3…

2…

1…

Pay Now!

Get ALL the KOHLs GIFTCARDS! #282708

To: *debradallas@aol.com*

From: *kohlsurprise@uigb.rus*

Subject: Get ALL the KOHLs GIFTCARDS! #282708

ACCOUNT User Your.Email@kohlsgiftcards.co

DO you have the Kohl's giftcards yet? Are you an ancient white woman who reads every single email? Sure!

GIFT NOW presents free Kohl's giftcards!

These are the best of the giftcards for a store you like, plus we heard grandchildren love Kohls.

Get a very cheap discount for $50 Kohls credit. All you have to do is take free survey by clicking on a harmless link!

PLEASE CLICK:

myxlqrxy.grtgk/us/kohls

Not a trick! Free ~ gift card~ !

You received this because your email address and credit card information have been leaked from Kohls.com

Best in Academia

In a country where fewer than one third of citizens hold a college degree, advanced learning can seem intimidating and appear closed off. But, behind the ivy walls of higher education lurk the same clueless authorities and lazy children trying their best to write an email that doesn't sound "dumb." They just wear sweaters.

Re: Paper Due

To: *jeong-davis@usc.edu*
From:*bcrawford@usc.edu*
Subject: Re: Paper Due

Hey Prof. Jeong-Davis,

Yeah thanks for the reminder about my paper on endocrine disruptors. I know it's due today. The truth right now is that it isn't done yet, and that's my bad.

So like, I CAN get it to you by tomorrow. It won't be in MLA format though. If you gave me a 3-day extension I could type it up and get it proofread, which I assume you'd prefer.

BUT, there's no way I could book enough lab time in just 3 days. How about a 5-day extension so I can book the lab time? Plus, as an added bonus, you'll also get my lab notes in the paper.

That SAID, it won't be enough time to check out those internal medicine books from the library. If I had a 9-day extension, I could have *just* enough time to check out and read some of the assigned books.

However – if you *need* me to cite the sources from my research, that will take another 3 days and an additional $500 sourcing fee.

Can we all just settle on a 1-year extension?

Also, Med school apps are due really soon, so could I get a quick letter of recommendation? It's due tomorrow, and that's a hard deadline.

On the first day of class, you said you were dedicated to teaching so please don't fuck up my future.

Hope you can help me out here!

Thank you in advance,

Bradley C.

Re: Psych presentation??

To: *psychstudyers@googlegroups.com*
From: *daisy.jackson.97@gmail.com*
Subject: Re: Psych presentation??

Hay guys!

Most of us on this project have a B at best, so Prof really wants to see us STEP IT THE F UP for this presentation. I already did all the chapter reading about the different personality disorders – here are all the props we'll need:

- Projector (in classroom?)

- White board (also in classroom?)

- White board markers (def in classroom)

- Fedoras (3)

- Live cat (from Dave's parents' house?)

- Astroturf

- Football helmets

- Pinball machine (broken)

- Pinball machine (70s)

- Pinball machine (critically-acclaimed)

- Bowl of fruit (stolen from cafeteria)

- Zoot suits (for boys)

- Ballroom dancing gowns (for gals)

- Umbrellas (5)

- Water hose

- Can of mixed nuts

- Zombie makeup pallette

- Pitchforks (3)

- Bale of hay

OK, who can get what? I can for sure get one of the umbrellas if I can get the next train out to my parents' house.

Lemme know asap!

<3 Daisy

PS: Which one of us has a car to pick up all the stuff? I'm morally against cars, so it has to be someone else. Morgan?

PPS: What day is the presentation again??

Best in Complaints

Times of crisis. Times of confusion. Times of indignation. These are the moments in which we must hold others accountable, speaking truth to power with the best tool we have as vigilant citizens of a democracy: the complaint email. The following emailers do not seek a solution. They just want to yell. Let them.

CABLE PROBLEM

To: *support@palink.com*
From: *georgemeyershaw@palink.com*
Subject: CABLE PROBLEM

Dear Sirs In Charge of TV,

I told this to all the men who were fixing my cable box last week, who told me to call tech support, who were NOT helpful, and finally they said I should email this address.

This is my twelfth and final attempt!

TV is nothing but bad and rude words. Why can't you get my TV to tell me, "Hello George, have a nice day!"? Instead of, "There is a new version of Samsoon HubTroller, would you like to update?"

Furthermore, your channel 7 weatherman keeps getting it wrong about when it will rain. I went to the park without an umbrella on Tuesday based on his bad advice! Get rid of him.

And please stop providing me all these insipid shows about overly made-up ladies yelling with wine !!

I can't even drink wine, due to all the holes in my organs!?

If you want to save a customer, you had better change up the programming to something <u>more appropriate</u>, such as:

1. Competitive fly fishing

2. Reruns of *NYPD Blue* (<u>except</u> the one with Sipowicz' butt)

3. History channel that only plays the Zapruder film on repeat !

4. Competitive fly fishing: youth finals

Please tell Greta Van Susteren I say hello. She's pretty and I like her.

Sincerely,

George Meyershaw
Citizen and Cable Subscriber
Warren, PA

BOYCOTT MONSTER HIGH!

To: *distribution@mattel.com*
From: *debrasoup@saviorlink.net*
Subject: BOYCOTT MONSTER HIGH!

Dear Board of Directors, Mattel:

I am very, very disappointed in MATTEL products lately. Your toys give girls unrealistic expectations that will lead them down a path of unhappiness. How could you encourage girls to achieve careers in science and engineering?! We just don't have the head for it!

Now, your MONSTER HIGH dolls are a whole new level of disgusting. These are too scary for little girls! Why make them so gray and pale that they are DEAD? This is not ok. What happened to these girls in middle school? In case you didn't realize, all aspirational female dolls should be WHITE but with a faint sunkissed glow. (But not too tan, so they don't look like an *ethnic*.)

My heart died when my precious, innocent, and Christ-loving, milky-white 7 y/o daughter told me she wanted a Monster High doll called "Stephan-eek! Screamface." I drove her straight to the child psychiatric center two towns over, and explained that her soul has been consumed with Satan's demons.

And somehow they told me that I am "abusive?"

Whatever happened to the Barbie dolls with a '50s soda fountain set like I had as a girl? She just liked to hang out by the jukebox in a poodle skirt, waiting for Ken to pick her up from a sock hop. The real Ken never arrived, but I learned very good "waiting patiently" skills. And look at me now: I married a man who picks me up from places all the time.

Don't you worry, I'm going to keep my sweet little daughter away from your horrid devil dolls.

Do NOT anger the One Million Moms!!

Sincerely,
Debra Soup

PS: In case you're wondering: I saved my own poodle skirt in a vacuum sealer, which my daughter will wear at her PURITY ceremony – or else!

Best in Politics

Politics is people. And people are nightmares. The political email must admonish, threaten, and shill its way toward a greater goal. (Greater goal TBD.) The following messages are excellent examples of the best a political email can provide its recipient: an empty gesture.

Every Dollar Counts

To: *noragupta@gmail.com*
From: *akindler@senate.gov*
Subject: Every Dollar Counts

Dear Constituents and Supporters,

Election Day is only a week away! Boy, did this campaign go fast.

Despite the rocky patches this campaign has faced, I am honored that you have stood by me. With your trust and support, I can campaign again and again, no matter how many times I lose.

We're in the home stretch, and I'm here to ask if you can help out just a little more.

By donating 20 dollars now, you'll send a message to those fat cats in Washington:

"It is perfectly understandable that an elected representative's love of jazz, the most American of art forms, would lead them to believe the 'Scat Camp' he attended was in celebration of the jazz genre, and not of a sexual nature.

"Anyone alluding to leaked pictures taken of a certain Republican politician appearing to play, sleep, and masturbate with human feces at a 'Scat Camp' should not be trusted or believed. Fake news!

"And if the alleged photos did exist, they should not prevent Representative Kindler from seeking public office, and they are also doctored. Let's focus on the real issues."

Whatever happens next week, I will always fight for what's best for Spring County.

Sincerely,

Rep. Kindler

Thanks for Signing MoveOn.org Petition: Keep Alaska Furry Free!!

To: *junolover49@alaska.gov*

From: *scared_fuzzy@ymail.com*

Subject: Thanks for Signing MoveOn.org Petition: Keep Alaska Furry Free!!

Thank you for signing my petition, Keep Alaska Furry Free!! This is how real change happens!

As of now, the petition has received 23 signatures! We need to show North West Furries that we stand by our principles: NO anthropomorphic mascot animal people in Alaska.

We don't need original cybergoth dog characters and actual Rescue Rangers characters "yiffing" (their word) all over each other in broad daylight. They tempt us to quit our jobs and engage in colorful furry sex all day with partners who are both open-minded and soft to the touch – disgraceful!

We need a lot more people to join in to make this a law. Click here to share on every Facebook shitposting group you know!

Thank you! And remember, God probably hates furries too.

—Sandra Perry, Community Organizer & Professional Browncoat

Best in Crowdfunding

Many artists say the most satisfying part of completing a creative project is knowing that the final product will make someone, somewhere, happy. In crowdfunding, the most satisfying part of completing a creative project is knowing that at the very least, your mom will kick in the final $3000 if you come up short. These emails capture the dizzying thrill of asking the internet for money.

Backer Update #1825: Ultra Skatefighter Go!

To: *AWESOMEBACKERS@googlegroups.com*
From: *megapixelent@pegamixel.com*
Subject: Backer Update #1825: Ultra Skatefighter Go!

Hey Everyone!

When we first launched the Kickstarter campaign for Ultra Skatefighter Go, we knew this would be PegaMixel's biggest challenge yet.

We set upon the seemingly impossible task of making the first-ever 3D open world platformer to combine brawling with skateboarding gameplay, and live action cut scenes, plus a 90 minute motion comic detailing the Ultra Skatefighting League's incredible mythology. We never backed down from that vision.

It was because of you, our awesome backers, that we not only overfunded by 40%, and earned over $43 million.It was also you who reminded us that we had a scheduled ship date of September 2010. How the time whizzes by!

There was an onslaught of unforeseen challenges we encountered during development: The voice actors went on strike, my buddy Mike suggested I hire 2D artists and use a Photoshop filter to make the illustrations look 3D (whoops!), and finally, I was forced to put myself through programming school to learn how a video game is made. Still, no regrets.

Flash forward to almost a decade later, and, wow. Our incredible journey has led us all to this point: The realization that the game doesn't need to be shipped.

That's because *Ultra Skatefighter Go* was in **you** the entire time.

It turns out you don't need to press X and down to do an ollie, because there's a D-Pad in your heart, and it's got the best rumble pack of them all. And when you close your eyes at night, you can see the most incredible cut scenes imaginable.

They're called *dreams*.

Good luck with the game your spirit and hope helped create. May the wish that MegaPixel could ever complete a project of this magnitude live on in your hearts. Now that we've fulfilled our obligation to you, I'll be using the remaining $1.3 million to ensure that I've learned my lesson.

Stay tuned for my next project: Ultra Space Shuttle Turbo, an Oculus Rift open world experience that actually works with the Space X Earth orbit program! We're all going to spaaaace!

Godspeed,

Chris Bolen
CEO/Producer/Programmer/Illustrator/Writer/Intern
PegaMixel Games

PS: No refunds!

GoFundMe: Sally Needs a New Car

To: *BESTIES!!!@googlegroups.com, and 286 others*
From: *canigetasuggestion@hotmail.com*
Subject: GoFundMe: Sally Needs a New Car

Hey Loved Ones,

I hope this finds you well, as I am not doing so great! In case you have not read my riveting 1,800-word Facebook post (234 total likes and reactions!) detailing the incident, my car was vandalized!

While I was touring The American Southwest to promote my one woman improv showcase, I ended up in a really shady place – New Mexico. I left my car parked on the main road where the bar I performed (brilliantly) in was located. My show is about the prejudice and discrimination that beautiful people from wealthy, connected families must face everyday.

When I returned, the car was graffitied with the words, "GO BACK TO LA YOU HACK" on the hood of my brand new hot pink 2016 Chevy Cruze.

I was humiliated, dismayed, horrified. Imagine me, driving all the way back home, all 679 miles, with *that* on my car. Not even the arid climes of The American Southwest could dry my tears.

I even bought spraypaint and tried to change the horrible slur to say, "GOAL BACK TO LAB YOUTUBE HACKYSACK!" But the original letters started to rub off. It turned out the message was written in chalk.

That's right, chalk! The ultimate mind game. Now, even though the words are no longer on my car, I can never forget them. They are still etched into my heart. As scars.

You might be thinking: "Maybe you should just go to therapy for a bit?" But I'm too scarred by the incident for even therapy. Would you be able to drive around, doing your daily business, all while knowing that someone had once done something mean to you? I'll always know. I don't need that kind of bad energy in my life. I'm already struggling to make it in The Business!

Time for a fresh start. That's why I started a GoFundMe page: gofundme.com/SallyNeedsANewCar?294t6

I hope you all find it in your hearts and wallets to help your beloved Sally in her darkest hour, so I can afford an even newer make and model with cool *features*! You know, to rub it in those vandals' faces.

All My Love,

Sally Drumlets
Comedienne & Storyteller

Best in Getting Rid of a Couch

Acquiring a new couch (or, "sofa," if you are insufferable) is an inevitable rite of passage as an adult. But, in the following emails, one chore stands in the way: getting rid of the old couch in a timely manner to ensure a smooth and secure transfer of power.

Amazing Almost Super New Sofa

To: *friendzzz@googlegroups.com*
From: *annieanddannyloveeachother@gmail.com*
Subject: Amazing Almost Super New Sofa

Hey Guys!

So excited that you're all coming to our Bungalow *Fungalow* housewarming party! Daniel and I can't wait to show you around the new bungalow, and how much more we've fallen in love since buying it. It's technically much smaller than our old apartment, but we own it!

So, we have to get a new couch. Sadly, that means we have to say goodbye to Old Faithful, the leather sofa you all know and love. It's in great condition and stuffed with love!

Since finding it on the street outside that frat house in 2001, there have been so many stories, so many memories in this couch: That time all us ladies did wine-stands (for the fellas: that's a keg stand with wine!), splashing the cushions with buttery chardonnay; the time our dog Maddie gave birth to a litter of beautiful puppies, soaking the flip-side of the cushions with her natural doggy mommy juices; when that squatter came into our apartment while we were on vaycay and carved the anarchy symbol into the armrest; when the cat made the sofa its bride; it's like a living record of all the best times!

THESE MEMORIES CAN ALL BE YOURS! We assure you there are NO fleas, carpet beetles, or bedbugs (that we haven't named)! You know us, you get it!

Below is a photo. If you want to grab it just call dibs, Venmo us $1000, and pick it up at the party!* Couch-a-bunga!

See you in our new bungalow! Bring galoshes, because there's a moat of mud surrounding the doorstep until we get the porch repaired!

Oh and FYI, our neighbors are Hispanic (or is it Latino? We'll ask them, a lot!), just so you're not surprised when you visit. :-)

Hearts,

<3 Annie + Danny

"Success occurs when your dreams become bigger than your excuses."
–American Proverb

Gotta couch?

To: *couchowner69@gmail.com*
From: *milomaniacr@ymail.com*
Subject: Gotta couch?

Hey dude i heard u got this legit midcentury milo baughman joint u wanna sell fr $4800 obo…… … i can pay u $124 fr it.

That's my offer…. .. hope u like it…. .. … . !

Это высококачественная программа фишинга, вся ваша информация теперь принадлежит мне и моей группе поддельных покупателей кушетки в Кремле. Вау вы американцы очень глупые ха-ха

[Editor's translation: This is high-quality phishing program. All your information now belongs to me and my group of fake couch buyers in the Kremlin. Wow, you Americans are very stupid.]

Best in Non-Apologies

A single earnest and heartfelt apology can end years of pain and suffering. So why give that up that sweet leverage? The petty response is, "You don't. Never do that." The following inauthentic apology emails showcase perfectly measured levels of spite and despondence.

About all that...

To: hearts420l@ymail.com
From: *prissytinnie@hotmail.com*
Subject: About all that...

Hey gurrl! Just wanted to let you know that I feel for you right now and I am totally bummed, re: what happened at drinks with Margot last nite! I was so NOT trying to throw you under the bus!

OF COURSE you don't **only** get out of bed to do edibles! Because like, I also do edibles (but while in the bath – a more luxe way, honestly). Anyway, you should self-care however you see fit. <3

OBVIOUSLY you aren't the "expert on one night stands." It was a joke! I would never slut shame, no matter how many randos you bone in the name of "sex positivity!" :-D

AND DUH, you don't "probz have an eating disorder!" I was probz projecting my insecurities on you, because whenever I see someone eat a mediterranean flatbread that fast I start worrying about their ketones!! I can't help that! Anyway, only your doctor can tell you that you have a binge problem. Not even me, your closest friend, who once saw you drink a smoothie with SORBET in it, which gave me nightmares for weeks. :-0

I LUV YOU GIRL! See you at the canyon on Sunday? I've got a brunch date but I'll cut it short for you <3 <3 <3

Hugz,
Tinnie Baby

Guess My "Privilege" Is Showing

To: *b0rgman@gmail.com*
From: *aisha.harman@gmail.com*
Subject: Guess My "Privilege" Is Showing

Hey Aisha,

I wanted to follow-up and see if everything was OK? You didn't respond to my last 305 messages. As a Male Feminist Ally, I work very hard to check my privilege and amplify the voices of the women around me. *Especially* when they're as cute as you :-)

I know all the "women" in the IT department (heh) are now spreading the same rumor: that I messaged them a lot, that I kept asking for sex, that I kept begging them to let me show my p3n1s. But I have to say it's all really *convenient.*

How predictable: A man who works in tech is a creep. I guess I've also "never had sex before," unless it's "a premeditated sexual assault," followed by "months of verbally abusive messages designed to gaslight and intimidate my female workmates."

Wow, this is a real paint-by-numbers smear job. When will all the cliched stereotypes stop? Who's being intellectually dishonest now?

Wow, really makes you think.

x Bry

Best in Entertainment

Glitz, glamour, guilt! The world of ~~exploitation~~ entertainment is a source of some of the most fascinating and poignant celebrity-free emails. You could say the laptop is the new silver screen! Everybody certainly is saying that, but that doesn't make it true.

You're Invited to a Screening of ~HOCKEY JERKS~

To: *amandasjunkmail@ymail.com*
From: *thescreenery@screenery.film*
Subject: You're Invited to a Screening of ~HOCKEY JERKS~

SCREENINGS' GREETINGS!

Hey [amandasjunkmail@ymail.com],

Thanks for participating with The Screenery! We'd like to invite you to a screening in your area of the upcoming feature film, Hockey Jerks! Here's all of the information you need to attend this screening:

HOCKEY JERKS
Wednesday, May 30 | Showtime: 5:30 PM
Sandstone TinyVision Theater | 30001 W. Olympic Boulevard
Los Angeles, CA 90031

Please be sure to arrive no later than 6:30 A.M., because seating is on a first-come, first-bribed basis.

This invitation is for you and a guest between the ages of 17-79. Unfortunately, we cannot admit anyone to this screening that is outside of this criteria, but do know that we will not ask for ID.

EVERYONE WHO ATTENDS THE SCREENING & COMPLETES A SHORT SURVEY AFTERWARD WILL RECEIVE TWO FREE INDIVIDUAL RAISINETS [NO SUBSTITUTIONS] TO ENJOY DURING THE SHOW.

If you have seen and enjoyed <u>at least 3 of the following films and TV shows</u> then please continue to the RSVP information below:

- Clerks - Clerks, the Animated Series - Zach and Miri Make a Porno - Zach and Miri Make a Porno: XXX Porn Parody - Gigli	- Gigli 2: Direct to DVD-li - Jay & Silent Bob Have Their Own TV Show Now - Any of the other good comedy movies by a down-to-Earth, nerdy filmmaker you forgot you loved!

To attend, please confirm via our website:
www.thescreenery.com/HJ/signups

For a description of **HOCKEY JERKS,** as well as its MPAA rating status, please see below. Thank you for participating with The Screenery, and we hope to see you at the tiny, unventilated black box we generously describe as a movie theater!

Description: You are invited to see Hockey Jerks, a top secret sports action nerd comedy dramedy partially-animated horror movie by one of Hollywood's greatest auteurs! You'll never guess the creative genius behind this film. Spoiler Alert: It's not who you think it is!

OK, fine. You already know it's Kevin Smith. You almost certainly figured that out immediately. But hear us out: it'll be different this time. **It HAS to be different this time.**

This movie has characters you will enjoy watching, and won't leave you with a feeling of emptiness and regret.

Also, all staff at this screening will sign an NDA – not for the film, but for the audience. No one currently employed or contracted by The Screenery will be allowed to disclose that you attended this screening. It will be between us. We'll take it to the grave.

However, a roundish guy with a goatee and a hockey jersey wearing a trench coat might be sitting next to you, staring at you, waiting and hoping for you to laugh. Please be a pal and laugh, OK?

MPAA Rating Status: The movie has not yet been rated but is assumed to be R. The studio cannot guarantee the rating that the film will ultimately receive. But it *is* Kevin Smith, so, you get it. There's a joke about Squirrel Girl's pussy in this film. He thinks she stores nuts in it, or something. The joke is gross and bad, but probably the only one like that, right?

You do not need to register to confirm for this screening. We honestly just respect your courage and optimism in these trying circumstances. Just enter your code below.

The **SWORN SECRECY CODE** for this screening is: **1205306V8==D~**

Snoochie Boochies! See you at the movies!

Re: First draft thoughts?

To: *mattycoolguy@mac.com*
From: *biancacortez@gmail.com*
Subject: Re: First draft thoughts?

Heyyyyyyy babe, thanks so much for asking me to read the first draft of your screenplay! Nobody likes criticism, but overall: I think it's terrific. Just like you! That said, I was wondering a few things...

General notes:

- Do we need a description of every female character's breasts? Do they all need to be sopping wet throughout the entire film?

- Why does every female character introduction include "and he could tell they wanted him?"

- Is the Bianca in this script supposed to be me?

- How did you know my cup size? j/c

Specific notes:

- Page 12: Was the red pill part of a meninist subtext? Are you a Meninist now?

- Page 22-56: I think all of this dialogue was taken directly from *Fight Club*. Easy mistake!

- Page 69: Cool that you had the hero call out that the page number was 69, funny

- 96: This lady character was described only as having "knockout titties." That can be a fun style choice, but does her name also have to be "Brassiere?"

- Page 102: The only black character in the movie talks in jive.

Anyway, you're probably a genius and I don't understand your vision, so please help me understand.

Thanks babe!

<3 Bianca

PS: Since I read your screenplay, will you help me scare the raccoon out of the kitchen cabinet? It's not glamorous, but it's super important!

Best in Fandom

How does one judge whether someone is a true fan? How does one judge whether someone's actions warrant a restraining order? How does a judge refrain from fanning themselves as they order lunch on a hot summer day? The emailers in the following correspondences seek to find out.

Factual Correction

To: *theladiesoftheviewthepodcast@facebook.com*
Cc: *help@mailchimp.com*
From: *umactually86@gmail.com*
Subject: Factual Correction

Hey The Ladies of The View: The Podcast!

I've been a big fan for a really, really long time. Like, since the very first Behar-vs-Behar segment. It's crazy how often Joy Behar contradicts herself. Can't get enough. Way better than The Ellen Heads podcast, which is trash.

I feel like you guys have such a good time being casual, off-the-cuff and fun — it's what I love about you guys. Seriously, keep up the good work, you guys.

But you guys, I wanted to bring up a small thing in your most recent episode. In #725, titled, "What Raven Said," at the 2:13:34 mark, Theresa (my 4th fave co-host of the podcast!) erroneously pronounced Duff's former Disney show's titular character, "Lizzy McGuire." It's actually *mick-gwire*, NOT "mack-gwire," as you guys said a bunch of times in one of your amazing non-*View* related tangents.

I just think that if you guys are going to record your freeform conversations about anything, you should do a lot of research. This sort of a mistake is the kind of sloppy podcast journalism I would expect from The Ellen Heads podcast, but not from you!

I love you guys and your dedication to being funny, having really cool branding, and of course, to watching and chronicling the greatest daytime gabfest in television history, *The View*.

I would hate to stop my listenership because the hosts keep slipping up. That would make both of us feel bad!

Stay awesome,

Danny S. in Portland, OR

Commission Art Request - yuriboi34

To: *fiverr@fiverr.com*
From: *yuriboi34@ymail.com*
Subject: Commission Art Request - yuriboi34

Can you pls draw a 8 x 11 watercolor commission of the following?

Characters: Sonic the Hedghog, Ghost Rider, Nermal (on-model from *The Garfield Show*), Dave (on-model from *Minions* ride at Universal Studios Orlando [not Hollywood!])

Action: Sonic is wearing the jacket from *Drive* and holds a chili dog you can tell he spent at least 30 rings on. He watches as Dave the Minion is in a diaper and sits on the flaming head of Ghost Rider, who's also in a diaper. Dave is turning bright red and crying tears of joy. Nermal is in a maternity dress standing next to Sonic, fondling and licking the tip of his chili dog. You can tell they all met at a Sonic restaurant, and that after this they'll be best friends for life, because they really need each other like I need them.

I can pay you $50 from the money I'll make selling my toenail clippings at DragonCon next month, but you have to include video of you drawing the piece for my private, personal records.

plz reply to confirm.
yuriboi34

Best in Chain Letters

Many years ago, in the ancient times of internet 1.0, there were messages passed down from our ancestors. These were chain letters. Superstition and poor reasoning skills converged to make this a giant among the many genres of email. Extended relatives, friends from high school, and coworkers you talk to once a week all descended upon your inbox with a mission for you: Find a new way to say, "Hmm, didn't see it. Maybe it went to spam?!"*

*For more, reference the book *The Best American Lies.*

LIBTURDS AT IT AGAIN

To: *truthseekersunite@googlegroups.com*
From: *stillhatehillary@yahoo.com*
Subject: LIBTURDS AT IT AGAIN

FORWARD THIS EMAIL IMMEDIATELY

We have it on good authority from close sources that George Soros is paying the so-called tolerant SJW left millennials to buy almond milk from all the grocery stores to manipulate the futures market!

What is almond milk? Who knows!! How do you get milk from a nut? With hopey-changey mumbo gumbo maybe? Satanic ritual? Feminist crystals?

You or I wouldn't know, but you know who would: the teen lizard lesbians of Solyndra!

Stormer friends, let's ruin some vegan SJW snowflakes's day!

Forward this email to at least 10 people today to spread the word: Boycott and destroy almond milk! Make those spoiled libturds broke! Triggered much, Betas?

WITHOUT GEORGE SOROS' MONEY THEY WILL ALL STARVE!

Not Another Chain Letter!

To: *clvictim@gmail.com*

From: *proudauntie@gmail.com*

Subject: Not Another Chain Letter!

*****YOU WILL DIE IF YOU DON'T FWD THIS MESSAGE TO 30 PEOPLE*****

LOL, just kidding! Just some chain letter humor. Chain letters are self-referential now! The internet has gotten very sophisticated.

Prove how unafraid you are of chain letters by forwarding this email to 30 Gmail users (YES, they have to be Gmail accounts! Hotmail and Yahoo don't count, guys) or else...

YOU WILL GET CHAIN LETTERS

EVERY DAY

FOR THE REST OF YOUR LIFE!!

And the emails will follow you to every new account you start! Hurry up, everyone!

XO,

Pammy

"I'm a fan of anything that tries to replace human contact."
–Sheldon, The Big Bang Theory

Best in Neighbors

Thin walls, short fences, tiny mailboxes, tandem parking spaces – the boundaries of civility – are stretched beyond our ability to accept. The following emails are prime examples of the struggles endemic to not being rich enough to live far, far, far away from other people.

Plant Damage - PLEASE OPEN

To: *grablecreek@googlegroups.com*
From: *joann1@hotmail.com*
Subject: Plant Damage - PLEASE OPEN

Everyone,

Emergency!!: I noticed the plants I care for on my front patio are starting to wilt and dry out! The flowers' petals are fluttering to the ground! I'm crying.

My flowers brighten the days of children andmake adults sneeze in delight. Healthy flowers means a healthy community!

I take such good care of my plants so you can all enjoy them. I feed them plant food and water. I even sing to them in a special frequency instructed by a growth guru, which keeps their chakras aligned. It's of utmost importance the chakras stay ALIGNED!

There's only one explanation: <u>YOU</u> are bringing bad vibrations and negative energy with you as you walk past <u>MY</u> home. My plants are very sensitive and can't endure human-grade misery!

I've even special-ordered crystals which cost me over $1500 and under $1700 for flora healing, but this takes time. I need to you help by being POSITIVE around my helpless plants.

What to STOP doing:

- Putting out cigarettes in my plants

- Pouring your inferior water into my plants when I'm on vacation (Kate I told you the pH has to be 6.324!)

- Walking too brusquely near my plants

- Talking too loud near my plants – this includes conversations about current events, as I am raising my plants as medieval

What to START doing:

- Humming and singing (only major keys) to encourage bud growth

- Using crystals that are compatible with my crystals so the energy waves don't cancel out

- Ask me about my plants more often

Please: I write to you as a fellow neighbor of Grablecreek Terrace, the best townhome community in eastern Kentucky. (Trust me, I've lived in A LOT of apartment complexes!) I BELIEVE in you!

Joann Blick
Unit #33

HOA Meeting Update:
New Dumpster

To: *8674gentryter_hoa@googlegroups.com*
From: *hoaprez@gmail.com*
Subject: HOA Meeting Update: New Dumpster

Dear Homeowners of Gentry Village!

As we discussed at the last HOA meeting (Danny and Molly we saw you weren't there, so listen up), we're sick and tired of the **smelly, ugly eyesore of a dumpster** the city of Willowbrook provides for our cul-de-sac. **Sure, it's free, until you think about it**: We are paying, not in just tax dollars, but in years taken off our lives due to potentially toxic smells and the emotional stress of looking at a rusty dumpster.

The HOA members in attendance unanimously decided to pool our HOA dollars together to commission an architect to design and build a beautiful new dumpster. A new dumpster that **reflects our values** as a condominium community for families and their small-to-medium sized dogs.

The modernist architecture firm Bergstrom-Warring has put in a bid for the work, and I have to say it's stunning. The new dumpster would have a self-cleaning function, spray its own signature perfume scent after each refuse deposit, and will boast a slick, aerodynamic design. There is talk of self-driving functionality as well. It is, in every sense of the term, what we would call a Dream Dumpster.

We've tabulated the costs, and it will cost upwards of $186,000 to commission this exciting dumpster project. This means **we will have to work together to make this Dream Dumpster a reality**.

Effective immediately, **your HOA dues have increased from $256/month to $2357/month.** This is, of course, temporary until the dumpster is paid for in approximately 8-12 years.

Congratulations to this community once again for another **smart decision!**

Best,

Georgia Smitty
HOA President
Gentry Village

Best in Accidental Reply-Alls

The horror. It can happen to anyone, at any time. It's irreversible. It's mortifying. All you can hope for is the mercy of your peers, which you know you do not deserve. These accidental reply-alls likely left their recipients with many re: re: unanswered questions.

Re: Re: Re: 11/22 Report

To: *jerry@taylorwisellp.com* and *103 others*
From: *jrodriguez@taylorwise.com*
Subject: Re: Re: Re: 11/22 Report

Alright Jerry, here's a photo of my crush. His name is Mike and I met him at the commissary in the next building over, but don't tell anyone! You can't meet him because he's still in Frankfurt on business and can't use Skype or anything – I asked!

--

Jacqueline Rodriguez
Accounting
Taylor Wise LLP.

Re: Re: Re: Re: New Carpool Rotation

To: *marion.kim@techsitereg.net and 46 others*
From: *julie.piper@techsitereg.net*
Subject: Re: Re: Re: Re: New Carpool Rotation

Here's what I hope happens to Marion...

----- previous message-----

To: julie.piper@techsitereg.net and 46 others
From: marion.kim@techsitereg.net
Subject: Re: Re: Re: New Carpool Rotation

Hi I hope everyone's having a neato Friday! Next week, we're starting a new carpool pick-up system! This month it's Julie's turn to pick-up cohorts in Zone 3 (from Euclid St up to Parker Ave). Thank you so much, Julie. Happy weekend to all!

-Marion

Best in Holidays

From Dr. Martin Luther King Jr. Day to Christmas, we love holidays for providing a meaningful escape from work for a few days. We also resent holidays for forcing us to spend time with family – the least optional people in our lives. Which email is worse to get: one from work or one from your step-sister-in-law about which gift cards to exchange? The answer is obviously both.

Merry Christmas from the Wickers!

To: *ourprecioussheep@googlegroups.com*
From: *wickawickawack@ymail.com*
Subject: Merry Christmas from the Wickers!

The Reason for the Season!

Merry Christmas (NOT Happy Holidays!) from the Wicker family! (Well, *almost* all of the Wicker family.) Enjoy this lovely new photo of us taken with our brand new, 8 megapixel digital camera (yes, even Braeden managed to keep still!).

That's right! Merry Christmas to you, even if you no longer fear God, like ALL of us used to. Even if you are childless or use-over-the-counter cold medicine, we still believe with all our hearts that our God, America's God, cares for you.

That's right, Kaylan – we're even wishing a Merry Christmas to you, even though you live in the filthy modern day Gomorrah that is Milwaukee. Please make room for your God. He gave his only son for **you**. Never forget the reason for the season!

We are praying for you.

Love,

The true Wickers (the ones who still believe in God): Dawna, Phil, Shelley, Emma, Braeden, Taylor, Morgan, and Tagg.

PS: And remember, if you die before us, we will do VERY religious things with your dead body, whether you want us to or not!

You're Invited to a Halloween Dance-travaganza!

To: *edgycovenofwitches@googlegroups.com*
From: *maidmurder@hotmail.com*
Subject: You're Invited to a Halloween Dance-travaganza!

Grab your spookiest costumes and hold on for dear life, because we're "executing" a crazy party! This year's Sydney Street Halloween Party is themed after the most terrifying movie of all-time: *Dancer in the Dark*! This haunting film starring Bjork, Catherine Deneuve, and at least one Skarsgård will get you in a brooding spirit for Halloween mischief! What is Freddy Krueger scared of? The way our justice system fails the less fortunate!

Arrive by 9pm to make it for the first of 8 musical numbers! Watch the "I've Seen it All" choreography video by my co-host April!

This party will *have* it all: blinding contacts so no one at the party can see, judgey movie theatre ushers watching you, and we hired a vaguely ethnic maid who we will wrongly accuse of murder! It's like a full-on murder mystery dinner with mandatory music numbers everyone has to learn, **plus** you already know the ending! So no need to "hang around" until it's over.

Click here to RSVP at webvite

Best in Death Threats

The dark side of love and intense fandom – the death threat – has become an art form in and of itself. These final emails are standard bearers of the perfect internet death threat, with just the right amounts of impotent rage and grammatical errors.

U better die dumb boy

To: *mikeyborn2011@gmail.com*
From: *idontevenwantajob!@gmail.com*
Subject: U better die dumb doy

Hey just found the Bad Hat Boy meme and spent three hours finding your personal email so I could share my important opinions with u!

U the 6 year old boy with the bad hat? IMHO it's not even that bad. It's just a propeller cap with camouflage. Camo saves lives on the battlefield! Why does everyone like you?! Your a lil baby cuck boy! I must prove.....

1. Bad Hat Kid is a false flag hoax!

2. Bad Hat Kid is not entertainment!

3. Bad Hat Kid doesn't deserve to live!

As you see, you are stupid 6 y/o boy, and I am a very smart grownup. I am right. I have a plan to dismantle your hold on America and it is this:

1. Create campaign of anti Bad Hat Boy memes

2. Use geotags to locate Bad Hat Boy

3. Kill Bad Hat Boy by locking in my dads shed for months

I will be celebrated. You'll see!

New Comment on Video: "Let's Play – Puzzle Buddies for iPad"

To: *justtryingtoexist@gmail.com*

From: *lazyrapejokes@gmail.com*

Subject: New Comment on Video: "Let's Play – Puzzle Buddies for iPad"

Like you can even reeelaly play a video game! Why do you even try to play the video game?! **BITCH**

You're not even good at the video game. Guess what? You were so bad we looked up ur username and found your info and WE DOXXED YOU Mwah hahahaha!!!

Xpect a hundred pizzas from every pizza place you ever heard of ! Animal control is on their way to pick U up! Ur mom is gonne be detained by ICE! well put micro cams in ur butt and make a new oculus rift game of ur stretched out butt! My drones are coming for U BTCH

guess what, we;re not even playing with you. Ur gonna die. we're gonna kill you BIG TIME, all us <u>good</u> video gamers.

Then u will learn to never play video games ever again – cuz you CAN'T LOL!!! Pls listen to me im sad

DIE U BCIHT

Notable Subject Lines

A great subject line can be many things: succinct, informative, leading, baiting, puzzling, enraging, mystifying, terrifying, enlightening, disheartening, and of course, deadly. Below are among my favorite subject lines encountered while compiling this edition of *The Best American Emails*.

- Re: Please Approve ASAP

- Fwd: Fwd: Fwd: Balls Blasted

- Mom was on HSN again

- Greyhound Bus Lines: Now with Fewer Decapitations!

- See the problematic tweets your friends faved on Twitter!

- Password again?

- Sign this document: freelance_agreement.pdf

- Zappos Here, Wonderin How You Been, Girl

- Fwd: Cool avocado trick

- Calendar Alert: Daylight Savings (the bad one)

- Casting Notice: Hundreds of Fat White Men Needed

- The fascinating history of olive oil [AD]

- Sign This Petition Because I'm Your Dad

- I'm moving! Wait don't delete, please help I beg of you–

Honorable Attachments

If a picture is worth a thousand words, then an email attachment that's a ZIP file of a picture would be worth 300 words, due to an average 30% file compression for ZIP files. Below are a few attachments I felt were truly worthy of my esteemed praise.

- 📎 does_this_make_u_hot.mpg
- 📎 itemizedsreceipts.zip
- 📎 super-incriminating-evidence-dont-open.xls
- 📎 pathetic_evernote_export.enex
- 📎 extremely-late&plaigiarized-history-paper.docx
- 📎 hilarious_editorial_cartoon_blackface.jpg
- 📎 freelance_contract_20dollars-SIGNED.pdf
- 📎 free_gift_card_malware.exe
- 📎 dope-ass-demo-song.mp3
- 📎 photo_of_baby_emotional_blackmail.jpg
- 📎 file.zip.exe.jpg.lol.doc.wtf.tar.gz.cool
- 📎 donkey_kong_country-cheat-codes.rtf
- 📎 printable-mapquest-directions-to-sedona.pdf
- 📎 hooters_logo_icon_attachment.png

Special Thanks

This very silly book wouldn't exist without the hilarious Devastator Press Author Corps, who are presently: Zachary Auburn, David Dolan, Alex Firer, Joan Ford, Jenny Jaffe, Kenny Keil, Lee Keeler, Asterios Kokkinos, Gabriel Laks, Michael Levine, Jamie Loftus, Hana Michels, and Julia Prescott.

Double thanks to Robin Higgins, Gabriel Laks, and Lesley Tsina, three of my favorite writers, for their extra guidance and funny jokes!

Triple thanks to my partner and editor Geoffrey Golden, for his wise notes and for pushing me to write dozens of goofy emails after so many long days of writing actual emails.

READ MORE
FUNNY BOOKS FROM

THE DEVASTATOR

devastatorpress.com